A Woodland
Counting Book
by Claudia McGehee

University of Iowa Press
Iowa City

University of Iowa Press, Iowa City 52242
Copyright © 2006 by Claudia McGehee
http://www.uiowapress.org
All rights reserved
Printed in China

Library of Congress Cataloging-in-Publication Data
McGehee, Claudia, 1963–.
A woodland counting book / Claudia McGehee.
p.   cm.— (A bur oak book)
ISBN 0-87745-989-4 (lib. bdg.)
1. Counting—Juvenile literature.   2. Forest plants—
Juvenile literature.   3. Forest animals—Juvenile literature.
I. Title.   II. Series.
QA113.M3935 2006   2006044597
513.2'11—dc22

06 07 08 09 10 C 5 4 3 2 1

To my parents, Carl and Pat, who have
always loved a walk in the woods

one white oak

two luna moths

three bobcats

four barred owls

five showy lady's-slippers

six pileated woodpeckers

seven gray foxes

eight mourning cloaks

nine blue spotted salamanders

ten rosyface shiners

eleven indigo buntings

12

twelve evening bats

13

thirteen serviceberries

fourteen wild turkeys

fifteen shagbark hickory nuts

16

sixteen black-capped chickadees

seventeen red squirrels

18

eighteen turkey tail fungi

19

nineteen orchard orioles

20

twenty gray treefrogs

thirty Dutchman's breeches

40

forty mayapples

fifty carpenter ants

one woodland community

Woodland Notes

Many people cherish a walk in the woods. The trill of a colorful song-bird, the rustle of a digging squirrel, the rough feel of tree bark surprise and delight us. In all seasons, woodlands are places of peaceful beauty.

Towering oak and hickory woodlands once fringed the tallgrass prairie of the Midwest. In a wondrous mixture of plant and animal life, big mammals like black bears and cougars thrived alongside gray foxes and ovenbirds.

The woodlands encountered by settlers in the early 1800s were open and parklike; fires set by native Americans and by lightning kept fast-growing shrubs and trees from overtaking slower-growing plants. But as more people arrived the woodlands, like the tallgrass prairie, were cleared with amazing speed. Now only small portions of this special habitat remain, and many of its animals and plants are endangered or extinct: gone forever.

Many people are working to restore and enlarge what remains so that woodlands can continue to support a rich wildlife community. In 2005, the rediscovery of the magnificent ivory-billed woodpecker, long thought to be extinct, in the Big Woods of Arkansas shows how important it is to conserve woodlands.

In these pages, we invite you to learn about many of the plants and animals that are part of the woodland family. From a single mighty oak to fifty carpenter ants, each mighty in its own way, every woodland member fills a special place in nature.

White oak, *Quercus alba*: The white oak is one of the woodlands' tallest citizens. It is an extremely important source of food and shelter for many animals. Acorns from oak trees are a big part of winter diets for animals from tiny mice to sizable deer. Some years, oak trees produce more acorns than usual—these are called mast years.

Luna moth, *Actias luna*: Luna moths fly only at night. One of the largest moths in North America, they have lovely pale green wings that spread over four inches wide, transparent eyespots on their wings, and curving kitelike tails. The males' antennae are larger and more feathery than those of the females. As caterpillars, they eat leaves from many woodland trees.

Bobcat, *Lynx rufus*: This shy wild feline, whose stubby bobbed tail provides its common name, is only a little larger than a house cat. Bobcats seek out rock shelters as dens where they raise their young. Once scarce, the bobcat is now more common in midwestern woodlands, although it prefers deeper, more northern forests.

Barred owl, *Strix varia*: Barred owls are bold birds that sometimes hunt during the day. Named for the brown and white bars on its chest, the barred owl is a fast, silent, and agile flyer with many distinctive hoots and calls. One hoot sounds like "Who cooks for you? Who cooks for you all?" Other calls sound like barking dogs or chattering monkeys.

Showy lady's-slipper, *Cypripedium reginae*: Also called the queen lady's-slipper, this wild orchid is a delicate sign of ancient moist woodlands. It may take more than ten years to produce its first flower. It is very rare and protected by law. Fortunately, unlike many other wild orchids, the showy lady's-slipper can be cultivated in greenhouses.

Pileated woodpecker, *Dryocopus pileatus*: This crow-size woodpecker is known for its flaming red crest; males have red mustaches as well. They prefer thick woodlands with older trees; look for their triangular nest holes in dead trees. Strong legs help them hang from the sides of trees, drumming with their beaks in search of insects. With well-developed vocal cords and the ability to drum and tap, woodpeckers are well equipped to communicate.

Gray fox, *Urocyon cinereoargenteus*: The gray fox is the only member of the dog family that can climb trees to forage for food or to escape from danger. Gray foxes are omnivorous; that is, they eat both plants and animals. Their diet varies according to each season—they will eat mice, voles, rabbits, nuts, berries, birds, and even insects.

Mourning cloak, *Nymphalis antiopa*: Often the first butterfly to be seen in the spring, this butterfly gets its name from the dark center area of its wings, which looks like a black funeral cloak. The underside of its wings is a dull brown, which makes these little butterflies blend into any woodland background.

Blue spotted salamander, *Ambystoma laterale*: Blue spotted salamanders like to hang out in moist woodland areas near ponds. When these little amphibians sense danger, they freeze, raise their tails straight up, and get ready to squirt an unpleasant-tasting liquid at any predator that comes too close. If an enemy grabs it, the salamander releases this defense liquid, detaches its tail—it can grow a new one—and slips away.

Rosyface shiner, *Notropis rubellus*: These minnows, found in calm woodland pools and streams, are schooling fish; they travel and lay their eggs in large groups. The head and front half of the body of adult males are orange to bright rosy red. Grown fish are only three inches long, small even for a minnow.

Indigo bunting, *Passerina cyanea*: Indigo buntings migrate from the tropics, more than a thousand miles away, to midwestern woodlands for spring mating season. They use the stars to help guide them during their night migrations. Adult male indigos are a brilliant blue in spring and summer and turn a cinnamon brown in the fall; females and young indigos are always brown.

Evening bat, *Nycticeius humeralis*: These small brown bats—their bodies are only as big as a mouse—have darker chocolate-colored faces, wings, and feet. They like to roost in hollow trees, not in caves like some bats. Females usually give birth to twin pups that are able to fly in about three weeks. Evening bats eat lots of flying insects; they use their wings like a tennis racket to bat their prey.

Serviceberries, *Amelanchier* species: Serviceberries grow on glossy green-leaved bushes and trees that bloom with dainty white star-shaped flowers in early spring. Their red summer fruits—sweeter than blueberries—turn dark purple in the fall and provide food for many animals and birds, including cedar waxwings, which will pass berries from one to another down a long row of birds.

Wild turkey, *Meleagris gallopavo*: Very communal, wild turkeys move about in small family flocks; they roost in trees at night. The iridescent-feathered males are called toms or gobblers, the less colorful females are hens, baby turkeys are poults, and a group of turkeys is a rafter. Surprisingly fast flyers, wild turkeys have been clocked at over 55 miles per hour. Like other game birds, they have special food storage pouches called crops near their throats; they can store seeds there for digestion later.

Shagbark hickory, *Carya ovata*: The distinctive shagbark hickory tree has a special bark; shaggy in appearance, it peels in long curly strips from the trunk and branches. The round, sectioned nuts are especially delicious to squirrels, but people enjoy them too. In the fall, shagbark hickory trees turn a brilliant gold.

Black-capped chickadee, *Poecile atricapilla*: These small, acrobatic songbirds may add extra "dee" notes to their famous "chick-a-dee-dee" call if a particularly dangerous enemy (like an owl) appears in the neighborhood. Chickadees are not shy at all; it is easy to observe them at feeders during the winter.

Red squirrel, *Tamiasciurus hudsonicus*: Abundant in woodlands, red squirrels live in nests on tree branches or in hollow trees; several may live in one nest together. They are active during all seasons but in severe weather they may stay in their nests for days. They store food in caches—hidden storage places—to return to later.

Turkey tail fungus, *Trametes versicolor*: The leathery turkey tail fungus grows on fallen logs and trees. Fungi are the major recyclers of the woodlands, helping decompose—break down—old or dead trees to create important nutrients for other plants and animals. Turkey tail "flowers" (the part you can see) form colorfully banded fans. The part you can't see grows underneath the bark, where it rots and recycles wood.

Orchard oriole, *Icterus spurius*: Orchard oriole males are a rich chestnut brown with a black hood; the females are a pale greenish yellow. Nesting in colonies in the same tree, they weave interesting cuplike hanging nests. Orchard orioles received their common name from their habit of nesting in cultivated fruit trees.

Gray treefrog, *Hyla versicolor*: Gray treefrogs breed around woodland ponds but spend most of their time in trees; their sticky toe pads make them good climbers. They can change color from bright green to gray to brown depending on their surroundings. In the spring, they lay floating egg clusters that are attached to plants on the water's surface. Treefrog tadpoles, with their distinctive reddish tails, emerge from these eggs in a few days.

Dutchman's breeches, *Dicentra cucullaria*: The single blooms of this small plant resemble a pair of white pants hanging upside down with their pockets out. One of the first flowers to appear each spring, Dutchman's breeches grow in older woodlands. Pioneer settlers called this plant staggerweed because if cattle ate its flowers, they became ill and unsteady on their feet.

Mayapple, *Podophyllum peltatum*: A spring wildflower, mayapples usually grow in groups. A shiny umbrella-like leaf hides a bowl-shaped white bloom underneath. Other names for this plant include hog apple, Indian apple, umbrella plant, wild lemon, and American mandrake. Like many woodland plants, the mayapple is poisonous.

Carpenter ant, *Camponotus pennsylvanicus*: Carpenter ants nest in many-roomed colonies; several thousand live together in hollow trees, rotten logs, or tree stumps. Some people think carpenter ants eat wood, but they actually only use it to construct their nests. Ants eat many different things but especially enjoy honeydew, a sweet liquid they collect from aphids, another woodland insect.

Woodland community: Woodlands are made up of layers of plant life. Each layer provides a special home for many different animals and plants, from the flying squirrel's nest high in a hollow tree to the underground burrow of the eastern mole far below. Together they create a healthy woodland community. Properly cared for by humans, woodlands will be safe homes for many generations of plants and animals to come.